preventing and managing disruptive passenger behaviour

A learning resource for airline crew to help them prevent and manage disruptive passenger behaviour.

SecuriCare International Limited

Martin House, Barley Rise, Strensall, York, England, YO32 5AA.
Telephone: +44 (0) 1904 492 442
Email: trainers@securicare.com
Website: www.securicare.com

ISBN: 978-0-9560159-3-8

Printed by Wood Richardson Ltd, Digital and Litho Printers,
Royden House, 156 Haxby Road, York, England, YO31 8EY

Copyright 2021. SecuriCare International limited.

All rights reserved. No part of this publication may be reproduced, stored in a retrieval system or transmitted in any form or by any means, electronic, mechanical, photocopying, recording, or otherwise, without prior permission of SecuriCare International Ltd.

Although great care has been taken in the production of this guidance to ensure accuracy, the Publishers cannot under any circumstances accept responsibility for errors, omissions, or advice given in this publication.

preventing and managing disruptive passenger behaviour

Authors
Philip N Hardy
Joanne Purvis
Adrian Pannett

Published by
SecuriCare International Ltd

CONTENTS:

Introduction
Defining Disruptive Behaviour
National and International Legislation
Understanding and Preventing Conflict
Communication Skills
Incident Management
De-escalation
Use of Force
Restraint Asphyxia
Post-Incident Procedures
Reflective Practice

Introduction

This learning resource is designed to provide Airline Crew with the knowledge and skills to prevent and manage disruptive passenger behaviour. This will help crew to interact with disruptive or even violent passengers positively, safely, and effectively.

The vast majority of passengers encountered will be happy to sit back, relax and enjoy the experience. Unfortunately, there will be occasions when some passengers may become distressed, frustrated, dissatisfied, and at times disruptive for a variety of reasons. These incidents have the potential to upset other passengers and will need to be managed by the crew; if they are not handled effectively, however, they can create feelings of anger, which could lead to aggressive or violent behaviour. This can disrupt the delivery of service and in many cases has been the cause of an unwanted and costly diversion. It is therefore essential that there is a carefully considered plan in place to help crew manage such eventualities in a positive way.

The content of this booklet has been developed with the assistance of airline professionals from many of the world's best-known airlines. Their input has provided a wealth of knowledge and experience based on the **real-life** management of disruptive passenger behaviour.

Defining Disruptive Behaviour

Disruptive behaviour on board an aircraft has been occurring since commercial flights started operating in the late 1920s. Thankfully, passengers that disrupt flights have always been in the minority and account for a very small percentage of overall passenger numbers. Internationally, disruptive passenger incidents occur approximately once in 1400 flights.

In the 1990s "AIR RAGE" hit the headlines following an increase in the number of recorded incidents. One headline reported a 400 % increase in incidents in one year. In truth, this was partly due to major changes in the reporting process, but nevertheless, incidents were more common as flying became cheaper and passenger numbers increased.

Media headlines and terms like "Air Rage" can be very emotive and can add to the fears and anxieties of some passengers and crew.

Disruptive behaviour can take on many forms and ranges from mildly annoying or irritating behaviours, to disruptive, violent, and potentially life-threatening incidents. Cabin Crew are the only available resource and have to be able to respond to and manage all types of behaviour, in addition to their many other responsibilities.

Air travel can be a joyful and exciting experience, unfortunately it can also be quite stressful and frustrating. The passengers overall experience from check-in to boarding the aircraft can involve both positive and negative experiences. The aircraft cabin is a truly unique environment and presents challenges of its own. We will consider the impact this can have on passenger behaviour later.

Air travel by its nature also presents challenges regarding the Law and, in particular, jurisdiction.

National and International Legislation

The airline industry has always operated under strict guidelines and legislation. In 1963 additional legislation was introduced to help with the management of disruptive passengers.

Tokyo Convention 1963 and Montreal Protocol 2014

The Tokyo Convention 1963 (amended by the Montreal Protocol 2014) is a modern and effective international legal framework for managing unruly and disruptive behaviour on board aircraft.

> The Tokyo Convention (1963), also known as The Convention on Offences and Certain Other Acts Committed on Board Aircraft, makes it unlawful to commit:
>
> *"Acts which, whether or not they are offences may or do jeopardize the safety of the aircraft or of persons or property therein or which jeopardize good order and discipline on board."*

Criminal offences committed on board international flights are governed by the Tokyo Convention 1963. It provides the guidelines for States to follow and provides the aircraft commanders with the power to take all reasonable steps, including restraint, to manage unruly passengers, to protect the safety of those on board, maintain discipline on the flight and to deliver the unruly passenger to law enforcement agents upon landing.

Jurisdiction

The need to establish jurisdiction and the powers to manage disruptive passenger incidents resulted in the formulation of the Tokyo Convention.
- An aircraft is considered to be in flight at any time from the moment when all its external doors are closed following embarkation until the moment when any such door is opened for disembarkation
- In the case of a forced landing, the flight shall be deemed to continue until competent authorities take over the responsibility for the aircraft and the persons and property on board
- When the State of the operator is not the same as the State of registration, the term "the State of registration", shall be deemed to be the State of the operator

Basically, the aircraft, people and property on board fall under the authority of the aircraft Commander from the moment the doors close until they are opened for disembarkation.

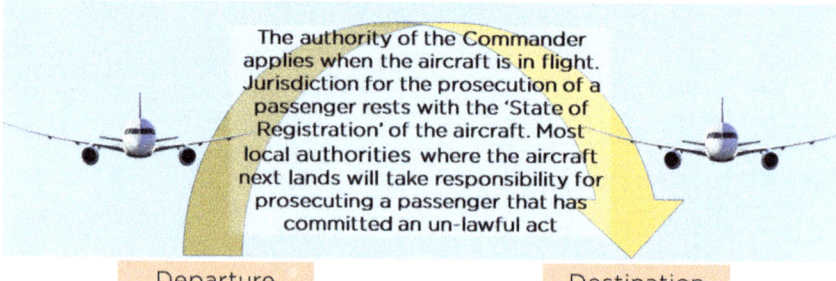

The authority of the Commander applies when the aircraft is in flight. Jurisdiction for the prosecution of a passenger rests with the 'State of Registration' of the aircraft. Most local authorities where the aircraft next lands will take responsibility for prosecuting a passenger that has committed an un-lawful act

Departure
The authority of the Commander applies when all external doors are closed.
In reality the local authorities would deal with any incident that took place whilst taxiing and before power is applied

Destination
The authority of the Commander still applies until the first door is opened for disembarkation.
In reality the local authorities would deal with any incident that took place once the aircraft has landed

The Aircraft Commander

The Commander shall be responsible for the safe operation of the aircraft and the safety of its occupants during flight.

In relation to the management of disruptive passengers the Flight Deck Crew no longer play any physical part. The risk to the overall safety of the aircraft and its occupants outweigh any need or desire they may feel to assist the Cabin Crew, however dangerous the crew's predicament.

Although not directly involved in the incident, the Commander still plays an important part in how the incident is managed and the actions and options available to the crew. The Commanders options include:
1. Divert the aircraft to the nearest airport and off-load the passenger
2. Arrange to hand the disruptive passenger over to the appropriate authorities on landing at the intended destination
3. Refuse the passenger any further carriage
4. Arrange prosecution of the passenger on return to the country of departure
5. Authorise crew to restrain the passenger for the remaining duration of the flight

The Power to Restrain

Most incidents can be resolved without the need for any physical and/or mechanical intervention, however, should this be required as a last resort, the legislation makes provision for the restraint of a passenger.

The Tokyo Convention confers powers upon the Commander of the aircraft who may, as a last resort, authorise the restraint of a passenger. *(Note: the Crew do not need the Commanders permission to use physical restraint but should seek permission to use mechanical restraint.)*

The convention states that: "An 'Aircraft Commander' who has reasonable grounds for believing that a person has committed, or is about to commit, on board his aircraft, an offence against the penal law of the State of Registration of the aircraft or a so-called 'jeopardising' act, may impose on that person such reasonable measures, including restraint, as are necessary:
- To protect the safety of the aircraft or of persons or property on board
- To maintain good order and discipline on board
- To enable him to disembark that person or to deliver him to the appropriate authorities"

The Power to Seek Assistance

An aircraft Commander may require or authorize the assistance of other crew members and may request or authorize, but not **require**, the assistance of in-flight security officers or other passengers to restrain any person whom he is entitled to restrain. Any crew member or passenger may also take reasonable preventive measures without such authorization when they have reasonable grounds to believe that such action is immediately necessary to protect the safety of the aircraft, or of persons or property therein.

Immunity from Suit

Following the protocols set out above, and acting in accordance with Article 10 of the Tokyo Convention, provides immunity from liability for those involved *(provided it is deemed that any force used was reasonable; see The Use of Force).*

International Civil Aviation Organisation

> Annex 17 to the International Civil Aviation Organisation (ICAO-2013) Chicago Convention (Convention on International Civil Aviation Security Safeguarding International Civil Aviation Against Acts of Unlawful Interference) defines a disruptive passenger as:
>
> *"A passenger who fails to respect the rules of conduct at an airport or on board an aircraft or to follow the instructions of the airport staff or crew members and thereby disturbs the good order and discipline at an airport or on board the aircraft."*

International Air Transport Association

The International Air Transport Association (IATA) developed a "non-exhaustive" list of examples of what is considered unruly or disruptive behaviour whilst on board an aircraft. This list includes:
- Refusal to comply with safety instructions (not following Cabin Crew requests such as direction to fasten a seat belt, to not smoke, to turn off a portable electronic device or by disrupting the safety announcements)
- Illegal consumption of narcotics
- Uncooperative passenger (examples include: interfering with the crew's duties, refusing to follow instructions to board or leave the aircraft)
- Verbal confrontation with Crew members or other passengers
- Physical confrontation with crew members or other passengers
- Making threats of any kind towards the crew, other passengers or the aircraft
- Sexual abuse/harassment
- Other type of riotous behaviour (examples include: screaming, annoying behaviour, kicking and banging heads on seat backs or tray tables)

Air Navigation Orders

Each country has its own legislation that define criminal acts on board an aircraft such as physical assault, sexual assault, damage to property and alcohol/drug misuse. There is also a body of Aviation law known collectively as the **Air Navigation Orders** that contain articles that explicitly outline the local definitions of "Jeopardising Acts". These articles are more or less the same across all legal jurisdictions, but for the purposes of this book we will use the UK Air Navigation Orders as an example:
- Article 240: "A person must not recklessly or negligently act in a manner likely to endanger the safety of an aircraft, or any person in an aircraft"
- Article 241: "A person must not recklessly or negligently cause or permit an aircraft to endanger any person or property"
- Article 242: "A person must not enter an aircraft when drunk, or be drunk in any aircraft"

- Article 243: "a person must not smoke in any compartment of an aircraft" – "at a time when smoking is prohibited"
- Article 244: "Every person in an aircraft must obey all lawful commands that the commander of that aircraft may give for the purposes of securing the safety of the aircraft and of the passenger and property carried therein, or the safety, efficiency or regulation of air navigation"
- Article 245: "No person shall while in an aircraft; use threatening, abusive or insulting words towards a member of the Crew of the aircraft; behave in a threatening, abusive, insulting or disorderly manner towards Crew of the aircraft; intentionally interfere with the performance by a member of the Crew of the aircraft of their duties"

Punishment and fines

Any passengers prosecuted for committing a jeopardising act on board an aircraft can expect to receive a punishment or fine as a result; in the United Kingdom the punishment for disruption varies depending on the severity of the event. Acts of drunkenness on an aircraft face a maximum fine of £5,000 and two year's imprisonment. The prison sentence for endangering the safety of an aircraft is up to five years. Disruptive passengers may also be asked to reimburse the airline for the cost of the diversion. Diversion costs typically range from £10,000 - £80,000 depending on the size of the aircraft and where it diverts to.

Four-Tier Threat Level Hierarchy

The International Civil Aviation Organisation (ICAO) have defined a four-tier threat level hierarchy. Although not all National Aviation Authorities follow these specific definitions, they provide valuable guidance to operators in determining the seriousness of an unruly passenger incident and in developing their policies and training for Crew in adopting an appropriate level of response. The ICAO level of threat hierarchy are as follows:

Level One: Disruptive Behaviour

Behavioural indicators include, but are not limited to:
- The use of unacceptable language towards a Crew member: swearing or use of profane language

- Unacceptable behaviour towards a crew member: communicating displeasure through tone of voice or rude gesture, provoking an argument or making unreasonable demands (e.g. refusal to give up on a denied request)
- A display of suspicious behaviour: e.g., agitated, numb, distant, and unresponsive behaviour
- Not following crew instructions or challenging authority
- Violation of a safety regulation

Level Two: Physically Abusive

Behavioural indicators include, but are not limited to:
- Physically abusive behaviour towards a crew member: openly or aggressively hostile action that includes a physical act of contact
- Obscene or lewd behaviour towards a crew member: actions of an overtly sexual, lecherous or lascivious nature

Level Three: Life Threatening Behaviour

Behavioural indicators include, but are not limited to:
- The threat, display, or use of a weapon
- Physical or sexual assault with intent to injure: violent, threatening, intimidating, or disorderly behaviour

Level Four: Attempted or Actual Breach of the Flight Deck

The highest level of threat includes, but is not limited to:
- An attempted or unauthorized intrusion into the flight deck
- A credible threat of death or serious bodily injury in an attempt to gain control of the aircraft
- Sabotage of or the attempt to sabotage the aircraft
- The display, use, or threat to use a weapon to breach the flight deck
- Actions that render the aircraft incapable of flight or that are likely to endanger its safety of flight
- Any attempt to unlawfully seize control of the aircraft

Police Protocols

Following a serious incident on board an aircraft, it is likely the flight crew will request the police or local authority to meet the aircraft on landing. If this is the case the police or local authority will require certain information so they are prepared to take an appropriate response.

What information is required prior to the aircraft landing?
- Where and when the incident happened; this may affect jurisdiction
- What type of incident has occurred and the level of threat it posed? E.g., smoking, a drunk passenger, a domestic incident, a passenger being physically aggressive or violent
- They will also want to know if the incident is still in progress or if it is under control, e.g., the passenger is restrained in their seat
- How many passengers are involved and what is their gender?
- Were any weapons involved to injure or threaten?
- Are there any injuries and is an ambulance required?
- Where will the aircraft go upon landing, e.g., which stand or pier?

What is expected of the cabin Crew after landing?
- Ensure all passengers remain seated when the aircraft pulls onto stand or pier and the doors are opened
- The senior crew member plus the best witness should fully appraise the police/authority
- Identify where the passenger is (seat number) and state their current mood
- Any evidence that may have been preserved must be handed to the police/authority
- Prevent any other witnesses from disembarking until the police/authority say it is OK for them to leave
- Ask everyone to be patient, as gathering evidence can take time

What are the key points to remember with regard to witnesses and evidence?

The following advice is offered:
- Record information as soon as is practically possible after the incident to improve accuracy
- Identify any key witnesses by name and seat number
- Record everything (do not edit); the police will decide what is and what is not applicable/relevant

- Make a note of any physical evidence found, how it was preserved, where it was stored and who it was handed to after landing
- It is also useful to note any circumstantial evidence. Whilst we may not have seen the passenger actually smoking, when the toilet was inspected after they vacated it a cigarette stub was found; this would be classed as circumstantial evidence
- Record direct speech (what was actually said)
- Keep all original notes
- Record descriptions of all persons involved in the incident (see Recording and Reporting)
- Consider making a sketch plan of the incident

Some additional advice:

We need to ensure that we only include what we witnessed in our statement. When we have given a statement to the police and the case is being heard in court, we need to ensure that we are familiar with the exact details of our statement and we should not elaborate or embellish upon that statement. Where possible, answer questions with a simple "**Yes**" or "**No**" as this reduces the risk of saying something that might provide an opportunity for further cross-examination.

If we are asked to identify an offender to the police, it is important to note in the statement that the police apprehended the identified individual and confirm that the individual is the same person who committed the offence. This will negate any argument that the police arrested the wrong person.

By following these procedures, the police should be provided with better evidence, which means it is more likely that the offenders will be prosecuted.

Understanding and Preventing Conflict

By far the best way to deal with difficult, unruly or disruptive passengers, is to make a positive intervention as early as possible. The earlier we deal with the underlying problem or frustration, the less chance there is of the behaviour escalating.

The vast majority of incidents we encounter on board the aircraft will fall into the level one disruptive behaviour category. How we respond to these behaviours will almost certainly determine whether or not the situation escalates or de-escalates. Our aim is to manage the incident effectively and efficiently so as to resolve the issue causing the behaviour in such a way that the passenger feels as though they have been treated fairly and honestly, even when the issue may be imaginary or the result of unrealistic expectations.

What a person thinks about the situation will affect how they feel, and if they feel strongly enough about the situation, this change in their emotional state can lead to a change in how they behave towards others. Their attitude and behaviour will in turn influence how others act and behave towards them; this is referred to as the Betari Box Theory and the following diagram is sometimes called the Betaris Box.

By positively changing our behaviour and attitude the behaviour of others will naturally change as well. Our feelings and attitude will directly influence our behaviour towards others, and this will affect how they feel and behave towards us. This emphasises the need to intervene in a positive way.

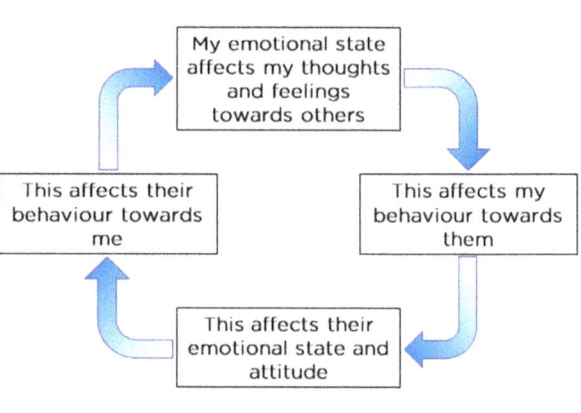

Understanding the Causes of Disruptive Behaviour

There will always be people who are difficult to interact with, but the majority of people are quite reasonable and only express negative feelings and behaviour when they feel upset, aggrieved or frustrated by their circumstances or someone else's attitude or actions.

How a person feels and responds to their circumstances can be the result of experiences and events that take place over hours, days, weeks, months, or even years. We are not usually in a position to help with the long-term influences affecting their current emotional or mental state, we can, however, help them through their current circumstances or issue. If we engage with the person with an empathic approach based on the assumption that their behaviour is only happening for a reason, we are much more likely to have a positive interaction.

It is worth keeping in mind that the passenger's journey to and through the airport can be a stressful experience and the thought of flying for some people can cause anxiety and fear. This, together with the everyday problems and frustrations people may encounter, can contribute to negative thoughts and behaviour.

The influencing factors that impact on people's thoughts and feelings (and therefore their behaviour) are either **permanent** or **temporary** factors.

Permanent factors are usually fixed and always have an influence, e.g., a person's education or "life-style" may make them more aggressive or less tolerant of others, or it could make them more affable and easy going.

Temporary factors can include an early start to the day, queues at check-in, security checks, lack of sleep, no seating available in departure lounges, other people's behaviour etc. There are also positive temporary factors that create positive feelings such as going on holiday, spending time with family and/or friends, and the experience of flying. These temporary factors come and go and only create temporary changes in mood or feelings.

Having made the distinction between permanent and temporary factors it is possible to break them down further into "**environmental**", "**organisational**" and "**personal**" factors.

It is the combination of all of these factors that can create the conditions for a confrontation if the person reaches the limit of their patience, they feel unjustly treated, or that the experience has not met their expectations (whether their expectations are realistic or not).

Influences on the Passenger's Feelings & Behaviour

Here are some examples of the different environmental, organisational and personal influencing factors:

Environmental Factors:
- Temporary: crowded or busy areas, long queues, no seating available, onboard seating issues, cabin temperature, unfamiliar environment, lack of luggage space
- Permanent: travelling to the airport, parking facilities and costs, distance between facilities, poor or dirty facilities, confusing signage, poor design (e.g. a lack of seating/space)

Organisational Factors:
- Temporary: waiting times, cancellations, delays, staffing problems, gate changes, boarding procedures, unavailable in-flight services
- Permanent: security checks, luggage restrictions, lack of resources, enforced operating procedures due to design faults, enforcing passenger safety

Personal Factors:
- Temporary: feeling uncomfortable or embarrassed, emotional stress, tiredness, pain, alcohol and/or drugs
- Permanent: personality, mental health issues, disabilities or difficulties that could prevent normal interaction/ communication, fear or phobia of flying, cultural differences

Given all the possible combinations of the above influencing factors, it is not hard to see why passengers may become stressed, frustrated, irritated and emotional. People sometimes have a genuine reason for being upset or angry, however, this does not justify aggressive, disruptive and certainly not violent behaviour

Patterns of Behaviour

There are some people who can go from calm to violent in a very short period; thankfully very few people fit this profile and most people follow a similar pattern of escalation as their feelings and behaviour change.

When people are in a state of calm, we normally find them easy to interact with, which makes communication easier. When someone is frustrated, agitated or angry, however, we need to think carefully about how we communicate with them. Events beyond our control may cause people's behaviour to escalate; this might mean the person is agitated or angry before we meet them. Most people's behaviour will not escalate any further than them becoming angry because of their ability to manage and regulate their behaviour, or because of the possible consequences that might arise if they allow their behaviour to escalate any further.

Violent

Threatening/ Aggressive

Abusive/ Non-compliant

Agitated/ Frustrated

Calm/Friendly

Having identified that a passenger is unhappy or angry, an early, positive intervention will make it easier to control events and de-escalate the situation. Remember, a person who has become angry and abusive may also take some time to return to a state of calm, so any further interaction will need to be carefully managed.

We should ensure that we do not expect, and therefore invite negative behaviour:
- Be non-judgemental and do not make assumptions about people just because of how they look or behave

- Remember, behaviour always happens for a reason, try to understand why the person is behaving as they are
- Believe that a positive outcome is possible
- Accept that mistakes can and do happen and that the person may have a genuine reason for being upset or angry
- Look for ways to rectify things in a positive way

Most incidents will be resolved amicably by communicating effectively with the passenger.

Communication Skills

Communicating with others is a skill that most of us use every day. Some people are better communicators than others, but the majority of us get it right most of the time. When communication fails people get confused, upset, frustrated or even angry.

Communication can be described as "the sharing of information" or "the imparting of a message", involving both a **transmitter** (the person sending the message) and a **receiver** (the person receiving the message).

How We Communicate

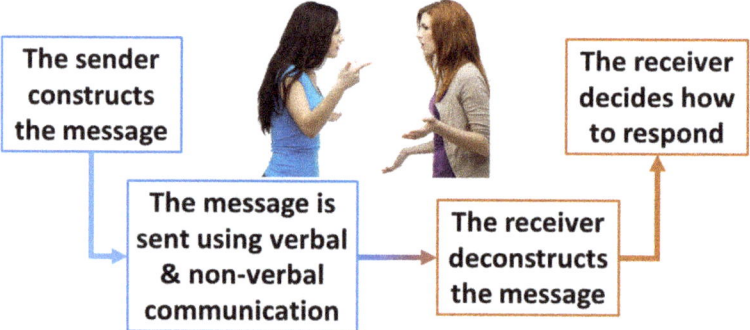

It's not what you say but HOW you say it!

Both the person "transmitting the message" and the person "receiving the message" will be subconsciously influenced by the others non-verbal communication as well as the content of the verbal message.

According to the British Journal of Social and Clinical Psychology, the messages we send are comprised of three parts: words, tone of voice, and body language.

This chart displays the influence that each of these parts plays in the communication process. This demonstrates that 93 % of the messages we transmit or receive is made up of body language and tone of voice. People will determine our true feelings towards them from how we appear and our tone of voice more than the actual words we speak.

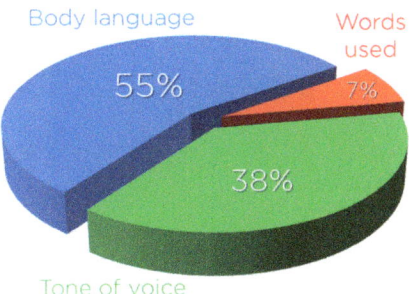

Source: British Journal of Clinical and Social Psychology

Body language or non-verbal communication includes:
- Facial expressions
- Eye contact
- Posture or stance
- Positioning of hands
- Personal space (proximity)
- Clothing or appearance
- Touch
- Gestures

When interacting with passengers we need to consider the effect that our body language and our presence is having. It is easy for the passenger to perceive you as aggressive if you are invading their personal space, which is easy to do in the confines of the cabin. When speaking, we must control our tone of voice and avoid raising our voice, or shouting, or talking too quickly.

Barriers to Communication

We may sometimes come up against barriers to communication; factors that the environment or individuals bring to the situation that has an impact on the communication process.

Barriers to communication fall into three main categories:

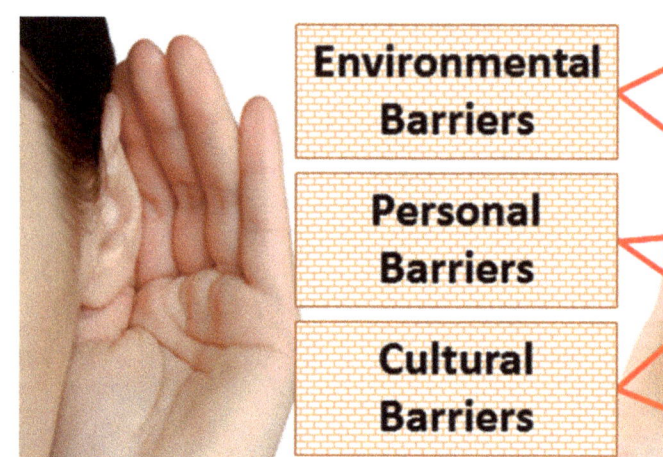
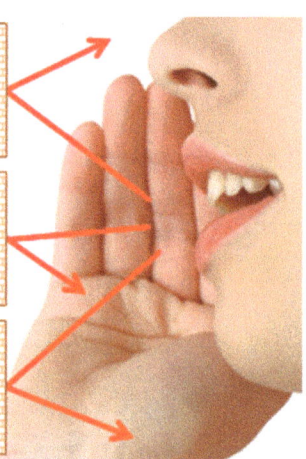

Environmental Barriers:
The setting within which the conversation is taking place can affect how successful the communication is. Environmental barriers include:
- The distance between the people trying to communicate
- Any physical barrier such as a screen or partition
- Lots of people talking at the same time
- The level of activity happening whilst we are trying to communicate
- Background noise/sounds
- Distractions
- Face masks/coverings
- Lighting

Personal Barriers:
Interpersonal and intrapersonal barriers refer to the human factors that could create a barrier to effective communication.

Interpersonal communication is between two or more people and relates to how well we communicate with others. It includes both verbal and non-verbal communication. It also involves listening and understanding the other person's perspective, how well we can problem solve and negotiate, and our ability to be assertive and make decisions.

Intrapersonal communication is between you and yourself and relates to emotional intelligence. It includes self-confidence and discipline, our self-awareness and how we conceive ourselves, our ability to concentrate and focus and overcome distractions.

Cultural Barriers:
Culture can be defined as "a particular social group or organisation characterised by a defined look, mind-set, attitude or behaviour". Cultural groups can be organised on the grounds of:
- Age
- Education
- Social status
- Race
- Religion
- Political beliefs
- Personal values
- Gender
- Economic position
- Health
- Beauty
- Popularity

Overcoming Barriers to Communication

The first step to overcoming barriers to communication is to ensure that we don't introduce any barriers ourselves.

Listening:
Active Listening involves more than just hearing the words a person is saying, it's also about being able to understand what the person means.

Not only do we need to listen, but we also need to be able to convince the other person that we are listening and understand what they are saying. A person is less likely to complain if we can demonstrate that we are listening, are interested in what they have to say, and they believe we are trying to help.

We need to allow the person time to explain their point of view without interrupting them, even if we don't agree with what they are saying. Often people simply need to talk to someone to help them release some internal frustration or anger. We should always focus on what they say, rather than how it makes us feel.

Asking Questions:
There are two types of questions that we can use: **Open** and **Closed**.

Open questions invite the person to communicate and express themselves. They ask the person to think and reflect, give their opinions and express their feelings.

Closed questions can be used to restrict the person's responses by limiting them to a simple "yes" or "no" answer, which can help us to control the tone and direction of the conversation. Closed questions allow us more time to speak and explain things in a calm, positive, and helpful manner.

Clarifying:
Using clarifying statements is a way of ensuring that everyone involved in the conversation understands the issues and the possible outcomes. They allow us to demonstrate that we have listened and are able to offer a solution

Summarising:
To conclude a conversation, we can summarise what has been discussed and the possible solutions, options, or outcomes available.

Despite our best efforts, there are times when these techniques fail to prevent the situation from escalating to a more hazardous level.

However, by attempting to communicate, by listening, and by demonstrating a willingness to help, our interaction should be seen as a positive one, which will if nothing else, promote positive witnessing.

Incident Management

There are common warning signs that a person is becoming agitated or angry, such as arguing or raising their voice, staring, suddenly standing, invading personal space or pushing and shoving. We also need to be aware of any sudden changes in mood or lack of responses to questions; sometimes a person may just go quiet or stop communicating.

Dealing with a high stress situation involving aggressive, threatening or violent passengers will have an additional impact on everyone involved.

Managing the Fight or Flight Response

When faced with angry or threatening behaviour, or asked to do something we may not be comfortable doing, we usually experience the effects of stress to some degree. The human body's natural response to stress is to either fight the threat or run away from it, hence the term "Fight or Flight".

The stress response is a primitive survival response that prepares us to act decisively to any developing danger or immediate perceived threat. It is a normal and natural response and can occur to differing degrees of intensity depending upon the situation and our past experiences.

The Effects of Stress

The symptoms of stress can be many and varied and they can affect people in many different ways. Some of the more common effects include:

Visual effects:
- Agitation
- Difficulty speaking
- Muscular tension
- Sweating
- Breathing faster

- Pupils dilate
- Shaking
- Red-faced

Hidden effects of Stress:
- Adrenaline rush
- Blood s diverted away from the digestive system, causing feelings of nausea or sickness
- Dry Mouth
- Loss or reduction of peripheral vision
- Heart rate increases
- Thinking becomes difficult or focused on the threat

Experiencing stress symptoms is not a sign of failure or an indication that we are not capable of performing our job, it is simply an indicator that we are dealing with a challenging or stressful situation and our body is registering and responding to this.

These changes are caused, in part, by the release of adrenaline into the bloodstream. One crucial effect this has is on our ability to reason with common sense. The brain finds it harder to control rational thought and is more prone to instinctive responses.

The key is to try to stay or at least appear, calm. The following techniques can be used to help manage the stress response.

Anticipate Difficulties:
With training and experience, we can learn to anticipate some of the difficulties and challenges that we could face and therefore be better prepared in the event of them occurring.

Controlled Breathing:
By taking a deep breath and breathing out slowly, we can reduce stress in two ways:
- It supplies the brain with more oxygen to help optimise thinking capacity
- The regulation of the breathing process will help to facilitate relaxation

Try to Relax Muscular Tension:
Muscular tension can promote negative thinking, which can result in the sustained release of stress hormones. By relaxing and loosening muscle tension we:
- Become more relaxed physically, which will help us to think more clearly
- Our body language will become more relaxed. This will mean the non-verbal signals we are sending out will be more conducive to calming and de-escalation

Mental Distance:
It is easy to become personally and emotionally involved in an incident, especially if the abuse or threats are directed towards us. We should:
- Try to keep a "mental distance" by focusing on the situation and solutions and not the behaviour and the people involved
- Remember, despite what they may be saying, we are probably not the cause of the person's change in mood or behaviour

Sometimes, after becoming personally and emotionally involved in a situation, it may be wise to let a colleague step in and take over. This will allow us to move away and allow a re-negotiation to begin. It may be the case that we are observing and supporting a colleague who is dealing with a difficult passenger and they have become personally and/or emotionally involved in an incident. By intervening and asking the passenger if there is anything we can do to assist, we might help deflect the passenger's attention away from our colleague, allowing them to step back both physically and mentally.

By working as a team and supporting each other in this way we will give everyone more confidence when dealing with stressful or volatile situations.

Dynamic Risk Assessment

When faced with a volatile situation, our ability to assess potential dangers can help reduce or eliminate the risks.

To help us to conduct a Dynamic Risk Assessment we can use the acronym **P.I.E.R.**:

P - People
- Does the behaviour of the passenger present a physical threat to anyone?
- Do they present a threat to the safety of the aircraft?

I - Items
- Are there any items or objects present that could become a threat or that could be used as a weapon?
- Are there other dangers such as bar carts, hot tea/coffee pots?

E - Environment
- Does the location of the incident present a hazard? E.g., in the galley or near a door
- Can we be seen by our colleagues?

R - Resources
- Are there other crew nearby that can be called upon for assistance and support?
- Is there a pre-planned response that can be implemented?

Assessing a situation gives you the opportunity to make choices and implement planned responses. The first option should always be to try to de-escalate the situation.

Effective De-escalation

To prevent further escalation we must be able to remain or at least appear calm. People who use aggressive or physically challenging behaviours to intimidate others, expect to provoke a reaction, either fear or aggression. If we can remain neutral and avoid either of these reactions it makes it more difficult for the aggressor to justify further aggression.

We can do this by allowing the passenger time or space and by moving away if necessary.

Adopt a relaxed and open posture by standing slightly to one side, at 45°, or approach from the rear of the seat. Our hands should be kept open and between us and the passenger. When talking remember to maintain an even tone and pitch and speak slowly.

The majority of situations in which we may become involved will end in a positive way. Our actions throughout should encourage positive witnessing. No one should be able to accuse us of making the situation any worse.

The Use of Force

Sometimes, through no fault of our own, incidents on board aircraft require crew to become physically involved.

It is important to remember that any action taken to prevent or manage abusive, threatening or violent behaviour will be judged on the following basis:

"was the action you took reasonable and necessary in all the circumstances?"

(Legal definitions with regards to the use of force are similar across all legal jurisdictions; for the purposes of this book we have used the UK definition as it appears in the Criminal Law Act 1967).

Section 3 Criminal Law Act 1967 states that:
"A person may use such force as is reasonable in the circumstances"

What is Reasonable and Necessary?

The use of force is only ever necessary if all other non-physical strategies have been exhausted or discounted.

Non-physical strategies may include:
- Asking the person to stop what they are doing
- Trying to resolve any conflict
- Removing or reducing any source of frustration
- Taking evasive action such as moving away

The use of force may be justified if it is being used:
- When acting to save a life or protect an individual from harm or danger
- When acting in self-defence
- To prevent a crime
- To protect property

Was the Force Used Proportionate?

The amount or degree of force required will depend on several factors, including:
- The size or strength differences between the people involved
- The number of people who are involved
- The presence of any weapons
- A direct or explicit threat to cause immediate harm
- An increase in the resistance or violence used
- An immediate threat to the safety of the aircraft
- An attempt to breach the flight deck

If the threat reduces or ceases then the amount of force used should also reduce or cease. Force should never be used as a form of punishment or in retribution.

Physical Action

Sudden unplanned responses to violent behaviour may include:
- Moving away or taking evasive action
- Limiting or preventing a person's movements
- Self-defence, e.g., blocking or holding
- Physically restraining a person, e.g., holding their arms
- Mechanical restraint, e.g., handcuffs or straps

Planned Physical Intervention

Through training and preparation, including techniques like role-playing, we can be better prepared to physically intervene in situations where the aircraft, crew or passengers need to be protected. Teamwork will be vital in these high-stress situations and there may be times when we need to accept assistance from passengers to gain control of a physically violent passenger.

Training and practice will be vital when restraint equipment such as handcuffs or straps are required. Crew should be trained to perform each role of an intervention where restraint equipment is used; in the limited space of the cabin, being able to reposition to perform a favoured role may not be possible.

The Risk of Asphyxia

The use of restrictive physical interventions and restraint equipment can increase the risk of asphyxia for the passenger being restrained.

There are two forms of Asphyxia:
- Positional Asphyxia occurs when the position of the individual prevents their respiratory system from functioning properly
- Restraint Asphyxia occurs when the position of the individual prevents their respiratory system from functioning properly and, because they are physical restrained, they cannot get out of that position

The Respiratory System

For a person's respiratory system to function they need the following 3 elements of anatomy to be free to work properly:

1. The Airway must be clear to allow oxygen in and out of the lungs.

2. The Chest must be able to expand to allow the lungs to inflate.

3. The Diaphragm has to be able to contract to increase lung capacity.

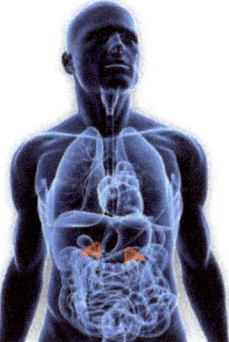

If one or more of these elements is compromised, the individual will either have difficulty taking in oxygen or difficulty expelling carbon dioxide and other gases, causing breathing difficulties.

Circumstances when asphyxia may occur are when an individual:
- Is laying down, either face-up or face-down, and pressure is applied to their head, neck, or torso
- Is bent forward whilst in a seated position, which can restrict movement of the diaphragm
- Has pressure applied to the head, neck, or torso during a restraint

- Has been mechanically restrained (belts, straps, handcuffs)
- Is confined in a position that restricts breathing and that they cannot escape from

There is an increased risk of asphyxia when:
- The person is intoxicated with alcohol, medication or drugs
- The person is suffering from respiratory problems or fatigue
- The person is overweight or overheated
- The person has previously exerted/exhausted themselves through violent activity such as struggling or fighting

What to look out for:
- Gurgling or gasping sounds
- Breathing that is laboured or distressed
- Verbal complaints or difficulty speaking
- An increased effort to struggle or distress/anxiety
- A violent or loud person suddenly changes to a passive, quiet and tranquil one
- Pale/grey/blue skin colouring to the lips, nail beds or earlobes, then to the face and other parts of the body

The risk of asphyxia can be reduced by:
- Avoiding applying direct pressure to the torso during restraint
- Moving a restrained individual to a seated, kneeling or standing position as soon as possible
- Reducing the level of intervention as soon as it is safe to do so
- Avoiding floor restraint where possible; in the close confines of the cabin it may be safer to release the person and re-engage with them in a less hazardous position
- Constantly monitoring the health of the individual and ensure they are never left unattended

If there is any reason to have concerns about the health of an individual seek immediate medical assistance and inform the flight deck.

Post-Incident

Immediately after an incident, whether the individual has been restrained or they have returned to a state of calm, it is important to maintain the safety of the aircraft, passengers and crew.

To do this we may need to do some or all of the following:
- Attend to any first aid concerns; where necessary seek medical assistance and inform the flight deck
- Comfort/reassure passengers who may have been or still are, affected by the behaviour of the disruptive passenger, which may be continuing
- As we start to calm after the incident the body will release noradrenaline, which will begin to counteract the effects of adrenaline; this can result in headaches, exhaustion, nausea, and possibly symptoms of shock for all those involved in the incident and those who witnessed it
- Provide as much information as possible to the flight deck and determine if a diversion is required
- Determine if the authorities are required to attend when you land (see Police Procedures)
- Collect/preserve any physical evidence

Recording and Reporting

Following any incident there will be a need to record what happened. A Disruptive Passenger Incident Report Form (DPIR) should be completed for all incidents, airline policies and procedures will need to be followed, and in some instances the authorities may require a witness statement.

Personal Recovery

Following involvement in a high-stress situation we may need time to return to our usual state of calm; this process can take longer for some and may involve a range of support measures. There is a practical, moral and legal requirement for employers to ensure that post incident procedures are available and accessible.

Available support can include:
- A team debrief to discuss the incident, including what went well and what didn't, but avoid discussing blame or criticising
- Time off or temporary change of responsibilities
- Professional counselling
- Restorative practices, used to help rebuild Crew relationships

Reflective Practice

In order to prevent similar incidents occurring in the future, we need to learn from past experiences; this will assist in implementing measures and training to eliminate the causes or triggers to these events, or to help crew respond more effectively when this kind of incident reoccurs.

There are various reflective models available, we can use elements of these models to learn from incidents on board aircraft. Here are the key points:

1. **What happened and why:**
   - Describe the incident in a chronological sequence
   - Identify what happened before the incident occurred
   - Who was involved?
   - What specifically, if anything, caused the incident?
   - Where did it occur?
   - What time did it occur?
   - Were there any other contributing factors?
2. **Analysis:**
   - What was your involvement or experience?
   - What did others do or experience?
   - What went well?
   - What did not go well?
   - What could have been done differently?
   - Do we need to change or amend the way things are done?
3. **Actions:**
   - Identify any additional training needs
   - Make necessary changes to policy or working practices
   - Review or introduce restrictions or penalties
4. **Evaluate:**
   - Have the actions taken made a difference?
   - Have incidents been reduced or eliminated?
   - Do crew feel safer and more capable?

Reflection can be a difficult process and some may find it uncomfortable, even distressing. The process should be focused on creating the opportunities to prevent incidents from reoccurring, help manage them better when they do reoccur or change what we do or how we do it to help keep everyone safe.

In Summary

People who present behaviours that are challenging, threatening or hazardous can be encountered anywhere and can be from any social, ethnic or economic group. The experience of flying and the unique environment of an aircraft bring an extra dimension to the problem of managing disruptive passengers or dangerous situations.

Legislation and penalties exist to deter most passengers from becoming disruptive or worse, however, a minority can go too far and create situations that require us to make difficult decisions and sometimes put ourselves at risk as a result. We hope the knowledge and advice offered in this book will help and support crew to manage disruptive passengers more effectively and help to keep everyone safe.

www.ingramcontent.com/pod-product-compliance
Lightning Source LLC
Chambersburg PA
CBHW062114290426
44110CB00023B/2813